Plan, Prepare, COOK

A Tasty Lunch

A⁺

Smart Apple Media

Contents

Published by Smart Apple Media,
an imprint of Black Rabbit Books
P.O. Box 3263, Mankato, Minnesota 56002
www.blackrabbitbooks.com

Printed in the United States of America by CG Books,
North Mankato, Minnesota.
PO1734
4-2015

Published by arrangement with the
Watts Publishing Group LTD, London.

Library of Congress Cataloging-in-Publication Data
Storey, Rita.
 A tasty lunch / Rita Storey.
    pages cm -- (Plan, prepare, cook)
Audience: Grades 4 to 6.
 Includes index.
 ISBN 978-1-59920-954-8
1. Cooking--Juvenile literature. 2. Luncheons--
Juvenile literature. I. Title.
 TX735.S785 2015
 641.5'3--dc23
                                          2013034430
Picture credits
All photographs Tudor Photography, Banbury, unless
otherwise stated. Bigstock p4; Shutterstock p5.

Cover images Tudor Photography
All photos posed by models. Thanks to Essen
Begum, Serena Clayton, and Emma Whitehouse.

Free activity sheets are available for pages marked with ⬇. Request them at info@blackrabbitbooks.com. Find out more on page 32.

Words in **bold** are in the glossary on page 30.

Before You Start

These simple rules will make sure you stay safe when you cook:

- Wash your hands before and after preparing food.
- Ask an adult to help when the recipe uses the oven or stovetop.
- If you have long hair, clip or tie it back.
- Dry your hands before you plug in or unplug any electrical appliances.
- Wear an apron or an old shirt.
- Wash up as you go along.
- Be extra careful with sharp knives.
- Ask an adult to help with the blender or food processor.
- Ask an adult to help you measure the ingredients.

Look for this useful guide to each recipe.

How long each recipe takes to make.

How difficult each recipe is to make.

Whether the recipe needs to be cooked.

All about Lunch

By lunchtime your body has used up the food you ate for breakfast. Lunch refuels your body until it is time for dinner.

Hot or Cold

Not everyone eats a hot meal at lunchtime. For a lot of people, lunch is a selection of cold foods packed at home and taken to school or work in a lunchbox. Cold food can be just as tasty as a hot meal—and just as good for you, too.

Fruit and Vegetables

You should eat at least five portions of fruit and vegetables every day (5-a-day). They should make up about one-third of what you eat. Frozen, canned, and dried fruits and vegetables all count. Try to eat lots of different colored fruits.

Meat, Fish, Chicken, Eggs, and Beans

These foods contain **protein**. Cooked meat and fish make good sandwich fillings (pages 8-9). Try adding them to a salad (pages 12-15) to make a complete meal that will keep you going until dinnertime.

Be Prepared

If you take a packed lunch to school, prepare as much as you can in advance. All the recipes in this book can be made the day before you eat them and kept in the fridge overnight.

The soup on pages 18-19 can be reheated in a pan. Pour the hot soup into a

This family is enjoying a healthy lunch with a variety of different foods.

thermos and you will have a delicious, warming meal waiting for you at lunchtime.

New Ideas

Planning, preparing, and cooking great-tasting lunches for yourself, friends, and family is great fun. You get to eat well, too!

Think of all the things you would like to make for lunch in the next week. Look through this book for some new ideas for recipes.

Make a shopping list of the things you need.

To eat a **balanced diet,** try not to eat the same foods every day. There are so many fun foods to choose from—try experimenting with some new tastes!

Go Shopping

Many people eat bread at lunchtime. There are a lot of different types of bread to choose from. They have a wide range of tastes and textures. Next time you visit a supermarket, see how many types you can find.

Whole wheat or **whole grain** bread is made from whole grain flour that contains all of the **grain** including the brown outer layer called the **bran layer**. It contains lots of **vitamins**, **minerals,** and **fiber**. As well as being good for you, it also has lots of flavor.

White bread is made from wheat that has had the bran layer removed.

Pita bread is a flat, oval bread which forms a pocket that can be filled.

This supermarket has a great variety of different types of bread to choose from.

Cheese and Yogurt

Cheese and yogurt are convenient foods to take in a lunchbox.
• Look at the labels on yogurts, and choose the ones lowest in sugar and fat.

Starchy Foods

You should eat **starchy** foods every day—they should make up about one third of what you eat. Examples include a portion of bread in sandwiches, or a rice or pasta salad.
• Choose whole grain or whole wheat varieties.
• For a sweet alternative, try the flapjack bars (pages 26–27). They are made from oats, which are another starchy food.

Labels

If you go shopping for food, look at the food labels. Some foods are very good for you. Foods that are high in salt, sugar, or **fat** are bad for you if you eat them too often.

• Look for **low-salt**, **low-sugar,** and **low-fat** foods (particularly if the fat is **saturated fat**) on food labels.

Supermarkets sell a wide range of foods made in handy sizes to put in lunchboxes. Many of these **processed foods** are high in sugar and fat. Some also have **artificial colorings** and **flavorings** to make them look more attractive. Eat them only very occasionally.

Chocolate bars and cookies are full of sugar. Take a fruity cup (see pages 22–23) or take some fresh fruit instead.

Water

You need water for your body to perform well. You get some water from the foods you eat. You should drink six to eight glasses of water a day—more in hot weather.

Sandwich Stacks

Have more than one filling in these sandwiches for more taste and goodness.

You Will Need

Cream Cheese and Celery:
- sharp knife
- cutting board
- mixing bowl
- tablespoon
- kitchen knife

Chicken Salad:
- sharp knife
- cutting board
- mixing bowl
- mixing spoon
- kitchen knife

Ingredients

- 3 small slices of bread—
  2 brown and 1 white
- small amount of butter
- 2 different fillings
Cream Cheese and Celery
- 1 stick celery
- 1 tablespoon cream cheese
Chicken Salad
- 1 piece cooked chicken (chopped)
- cucumber (chopped)
- 1 torn-up lettuce leaf

For more ideas for fillings see pages 10–11.

Prepare the Fillings

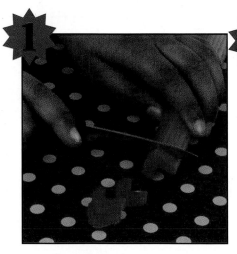

Cream Cheese and Celery
- Slice the celery (see page 29).

- In a bowl, mix celery with a tablespoon of cream cheese.

Chicken Salad
- In a bowl, mix the chicken, cucumber, and lettuce together.

- Butter both sides of the slice of white bread with the kitchen knife.
- Butter one side of each of the slices of brown bread.

- Place one slice of brown bread, butter-side up, on the cutting board.
- Spread the first filling on top.

- Put the white slice of bread on top of that.
- Cover with the second filling.

- Top with the last slice of brown bread.
- Cut into halves or quarters.

Tasty!

15 minutes

Easy

No cooking

9

Fishy Pitas

Pita breads are oval-shaped, flat breads. They make a perfect pocket to stuff with your favorite filling.

Ingredients

- small can of tuna fish in water or sunflower oil (drained)
- 1 tablespoon mayonnaise
- 1 large or 2 small pita breads
- small amount of butter
- some shredded lettuce
- sliced tomato

You Will Need

- bowl
- fork
- tablespoon
- sharp knife
- kitchen knife
- plate

Fish

Fish is a good source of protein, vitamins, and minerals. You should try to eat a portion of fish at least twice a week.

- Put the tuna fish into a bowl.
- Break it up with a fork.
- Add a tablespoon of mayonnaise and mix together.

- With a sharp knife, make a small cut in the side of the pita bread. Open it up to make a pocket.

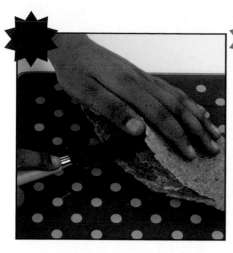

- Spread a little butter inside.

- Put the shredded lettuce into the bottom of the pocket.

- Put the tomato slices on top of the lettuce.

- Put spoonfuls of the filling on top of the lettuce and tomato.

Handy Hint

Canned salmon, smoked mackerel, or cooked fresh salmon or tuna will all work well as fishy fillings for your pita bread.

Delish!

15 minutes

Easy

No cooking

Rice Salad

Ingredients

- ½ cup (100 g.) brown rice
- 2 tablespoons of any of the following: chopped red pepper (see page 28), cooked green beans, corn, or peas
- 2 tablespoons chopped chicken
- 1½ tablespoons olive oil

This is enough for two servings.

Try this colorful chicken and rice salad instead of a sandwich at lunchtime. It is easy to pack into a container in your lunchbox.

Rice

Rice is a starchy food (see page 7). It gives you energy. Unlike white rice, brown rice has not had the outer bran layer removed. This means that as well as having more flavor, brown rice contains more vitamins, minerals, and fiber than white rice.

You Will Need

- a small saucepan
- colander
- mixing bowl
- measuring spoons
- measuring cups

1.
- Put the rice into the saucepan.
- Cover it with water.
- Put the saucepan on the burner and turn the burner on to high.

2.
- When the water is **boiling**, turn the heat down to medium. Cook for the time given on the box.
- Drain the rice in a colander placed in the sink.
- Remember to turn the burner off.

- Put the drained rice into a bowl and let cool.
- When the rice is cool, add all the other ingredients.

- Mix everything together.
- Put a serving into a bowl.

- If you are taking the salad in your lunchbox, pack it in a plastic container with a lid. Remember to include a fork!

Mmm!

Cool It!

Fill a small plastic bottle with water, leaving a gap at the top. Place it in the freezer overnight. In the morning, put it into a plastic bag in your lunchbox. By lunchtime you will have a cold drink—and your food will be cool too.

40 minutes

Medium

Cooked

13

Salad Layers

What you put in a salad bowl is up to you. Choose from the ingredients below, and make up your own favorite salad.

Grapes
Cut in half

Bottom Layer

Choose from:

Tomato
Sliced

Cucumber
Chopped

Corn

Celery
Sliced

Green onions
Sliced

Lettuce
Shredded

Red Pepper
Chopped

Top Layer
Choose from:

Chicken
Chopped into chunks

Shrimp

Hard-Boiled Egg
Sliced

Ham
Cut into strips

Tuna Fish
Flaked

Cheese
Cubed or grated (see page 29).

Beautiful!

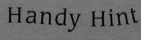

Handy Hint
To make a creamy salad dressing, mix a tablespoon of yogurt with a few chopped chives and a squirt of lemon juice.

Handy Hint
A few pumpkin or sunflower seeds sprinkled on a salad will add some extra crunch!

30 minutes

Easy

No cooking

Tortilla Wrap

Tortilla wraps are available in supermarkets. They are a good way to wrap up your favorite filling for lunch.

You Will Need

- kitchen knife
- tablespoon
- plate

Ingredients

- 1 tortilla
- 2 tablespoons cream cheese or sour cream
- cucumber slices (see page 29)
- tomato slices
- 1 tablespoon hummus

Beans

Beans are a starchy food that also contain fiber and protein. They are a good source of protein for people who do not eat meat. Three heaped tablespoons of beans also count as one of your 5-a-day (see page 4).

Hummus is made from beans called chickpeas. It can be bought in supermarkets. Some varieties are high in fat and salt, so check the label.

- Spread the cream cheese or sour cream over the middle of the tortilla.

- Add a layer of cucumber slices.

- Add a layer of tomato slices.

- Add a tablespoon of hummus.

- Fold in one edge of the tortilla as shown above.

- Fold in the second edge as shown above.

- Fold the top down to the middle.

- Cut into two pieces diagonally.

Yummy!

- Turn and fold the bottom to the middle.

15 minutes

Easy

No cooking

Vegetable Soup

This velvety-smooth soup is easy to make and full of tasty vegetables.

1

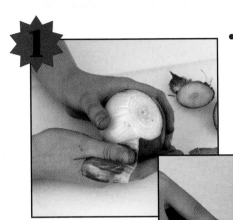

• Peel and chop the onion (see page 28).

Ingredients

• 1 onion
• 2 large carrots
• 1 stalk celery
• 1 tablespoon cooking oil
• 2 cups (600 ml) chicken or vegetable stock

You Will Need

• small sharp knife
• peeler
• cutting board
• saucepan
• wooden spoon
• measuring cup
• blender
• bowl

2

• Peel and slice the carrots (see page 29).

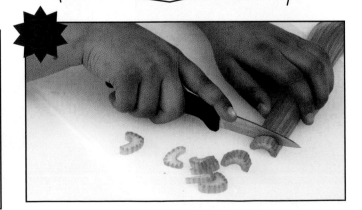

• Slice the stalk of celery.

- Turn the burner on to medium heat.
- Put the oil into the pan. Add the vegetables.
- Turn the heat down to low and keep stirring for 5 minutes.

- Add the stock to the vegetables in the pan.
- Cook for 15-20 minutes, or until the vegetables are soft.

- Put the stock and cooked vegetables into a blender and blend until the mixture is smooth.

- Pour the soup back into the pan and heat until almost boiling.
- Remember to turn the burner off.

- Serve with a thick slice of whole wheat bread.

Vegelicious!

30 minutes

Medium

Cooked

Omelet Slices

This thick Spanish-style omelet is delicious hot or cold. Serve it hot for a main meal, and leave a couple of slices in the fridge for your lunchbox.

Ingredients
- 2 medium potatoes
- 1 tablespoon oil
- 1 onion, chopped (see page 28)
- 3 eggs
- few strips red pepper (optional)

You Will Need
- peeler
- sharp knife
- cutting board
- frying pan
- spatula
- small bowl and fork

1

- Peel the potatoes with the peeler (see page 28).

2

- Cut the potatoes into slices.
- Cut the slices into sticks and then into cubes (see page 28).

3

- Put the oil in the frying pan. Place the pan on the burner on medium heat.
- Put the chopped onion and potato cubes in the pan. Add the red pepper if you are including it.

4

- Let them cook for about 15 minutes, or until the potatoes break up easily when you press them with the spatula.

- Crack the eggs into a bowl (see page 29).
- Mix well with a fork.

- Pour the beaten eggs on top of the cooked potatoes and onions.
- Cook over a low heat for 10 minutes.

- Flip the omelet over with a spatula (ask an adult to help).
- Cook for another minute.
- Remember to turn the burner off.

- Slide the omelet on to a plate.
- Cut into slices and enjoy it hot, or leave to cool.

Eggytastic!

Handy Hint

If you have any leftover vegetables—such as onions or zucchini—you could chop them up and add them to the potato and onion.

30 minutes

Tricky!

Cooked

Fruity Cups

Fruity cups can be made using any fruits that you have available. Use some unusual tropical fruits, or mix lots of different colors.

You Will Need

- small sharp knife
- bowl
- 4 glasses or a serving bowl
- measuring cup
- tablespoon

Ingredients

- 2 envelopes **gelatin**
- 2 cups (300 g.) strawberries and raspberries, washed and cut into pieces
- ½ cup (120 ml) boiling water
- 3 cups (700 ml) cranberry, grape, or raspberry juice

If You Prefer

To make a tropical cup, use orange segments, mango, and pineapple (canned, not fresh) with apple juice.

For a "tutti-frutti" cup, use as many different-colored fruits as you can with white grape juice.

- Divide the fruit pieces between the four glasses, or put them in the serving bowl.

- Put the gelatin into a glass measuring cup. Pour the boiling water over it.

- Stir until the gelatin has melted into the water.

- Add the fruit juice and stir to make a fruit jelly mixture.

- Pour the jelly over the fruit in the glasses or serving bowl.
- Leave to set in the fridge for a couple of hours.

More about 5-a-Day

It is recommended that you eat at least five servings (about ½ cup or 75 g.) of fruit and vegetables every day.

A serving is:

- One large fruit such as an apple, banana, orange, or pear.
- One slice of a very large fruit, such as a melon or pineapple.
- A handful of dried fruit or small fruits such as cherries, strawberries, or grapes.

Canned and frozen fruits count too.

- If you are putting a fruity cup into a lunchbox, make it in a plastic container that has a lid. To keep it cool, see the "Cool It!" tip on page 13.

Wow!

20 minutes

Easy

No cooking

Crispy Chocolate Cakes

These delicious, sweet treats are very easy to make. By adding the dried fruit, they can also be one of your 5-a-day. They are perfect as a lunchbox treat.

You Will Need

- saucepan and a bowl that fits on the top of the saucepan
- wooden spoon
- 12 cupcake liners
- teaspoon

Ingredients

- 8 oz (225 g.) chocolate bar
- 1¼ cup (300 ml) water
- 4 cups (960 g.) crisped rice
- ⅓ cup (50 g.) dried fruits such as raisins, cherries, and cranberries, or chopped nuts or coconut.

- Break the chocolate up into pieces and put the pieces into the bowl.

- Pour the water into the saucepan and place the pan on the burner. Turn the burner on to medium heat.

- Place the bowl on top of the saucepan. Stir the chocolate with a wooden spoon until it melts.
- Remember to turn the burner off.

4

- Take the bowl off the pan.
- Mix in the cereal and dried fruit.

- Spoon the mixture into the cupcake liners.
- Leave the cakes to cool in the fridge.

Yum!

30 minutes

Medium

Cooked

Oat Flapjack Bars

Oats are a good starchy food that will keep you from feeling hungry in the afternoon.

Before You Start

- Turn the oven on to 350°F (180° C).

You Will Need

- small saucepan
- wooden spoon
- non-stick baking pan (8 x 8 inches)
- kitchen knife
- wire cooling rack

Ingredients

- ½ cup (120 g.) butter (or one stick)
- ¼ cup (50 ml) light corn syrup
- ⅓ cup (60 g.) packed brown sugar
- 3 cups (270 g.) rolled oats

1

- Put the butter into the saucepan.

2

- Add the corn syrup and brown sugar.
- Turn the burner on to low.

- Heat the butter, syrup, and sugar until they have melted.
- Remember to turn the burner off.
- Add the oats to the saucepan, and stir them in with the wooden spoon.

- Pour the mixture into the pan.

- Smooth out with a kitchen knife.
- Bake in the preheated oven for 30 minutes.

- Take out of the oven and place the pan on the wire cooling rack.
- Cut into squares.
- Take the oat flapjack bars out of the pan when they are cold.

Sweeeeet!

1 hour

Medium

Cooked

Peel

To peel means to take off a small amount of the outside or skin of a fruit or vegetable.

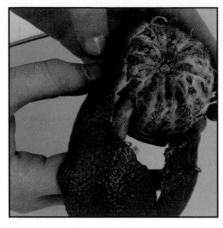

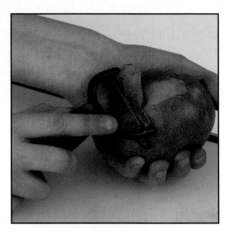

- Oranges have a thick peel. It is quite easy to take off with your fingers.

- To take the peel off potatoes, carrots, or kiwi fruits, it is safer to use a peeler than a knife.

Chop

Chopping is cutting something into lots of equal-sized pieces. How small the pieces are depends on what you are cooking. Nuts, fruits, vegetables, and meat can all be chopped.

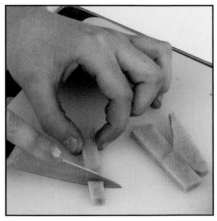

- Some things such as nuts need to be chopped very finely. You can do this in a food processor or blender.

- To chop into larger chunks called cubes, first take off a thick slice. Cut the slice into pieces first one way, and then the other.

Slice

Slicing is preparing something by cutting a thin piece from it. Bread, cheese, cucumber, tomatoes, fruits, vegetables, and meat can all be sliced.

- Hold the food firmly. Do not hold too close to the end you are cutting.
- Cut across the food using a sawing action.

Grate

A food grater has lots of sharp blades that can turn food into strips.

A box grater has different-sized blades for different foods.

Cheese and carrots are best grated on the coarsest blades.

- Press the food against the blades and push down.

Crack Open an Egg

1

2

3

- Tap the egg gently on the side of a bowl so that it cracks.
- Put your thumbs on either side of the crack.
- Hold the egg over the bowl and gently pull the shell apart.

29

Glossary

artificial coloring Man-made coloring added to food.

artificial flavoring Man-made flavors added to food.

balanced diet A diet that contains all the foods necessary to grow and stay healthy.

boiling The point when a liquid becomes hot enough to make large bubbles that rise to the surface and break.

bran layer The hard outer layer of grain. It contains fiber, vitamins, and minerals.

fat A greasy substance found in food. Fats are divided into two types: **saturated fats** are found in cream, cheese, butter, fatty meat, and chocolate; **unsaturated fats** are found in avocados, nuts, vegetable oils, and olive oils. Unsaturated fats are healthier than saturated fats.

fiber The part of a fruit or vegetable that cannot be digested. Fiber helps other food to be digested.

gelatin A setting agent used to make jellies. Some gelatin is suitable for vegetarians. Check the label on the package.

grain The starch seed of a plant such as wheat, corn, oats, or rice.

low-fat Describes a food that does not contain a lot of fat.

low-salt Describes a food that does not contain a lot of salt.

low-sugar Describes a food that does not contain a lot of sugar.

mineral A substance such as iron or calcium that the body needs to function properly. Minerals are found in foods.

pita bread A flat, oval bread which forms a pocket that can be filled.

processed food Any food product that has been changed in some way. Cooking, freezing, drying, canning, and preserving are all methods of processing food. Processed foods may contain colorings, flavorings, and other additives and preservatives.

protein A substance found in some foods. It is needed by the body to grow and develop properly. Meat, eggs, milk, and some types of beans contain protein.

starchy Describes a food containing starch. Starchy foods make up one of the food groups. They include foods such as bread, cereals, rice, pasta, and potatoes.

thermos A container that has double walls, used for keeping liquids hot or cold.

vitamin One of the substances that are essential in very small amounts in the body for normal growth and activity.

whole grain Describes cereals such as wheat, barley, and oats that have not had the outer layer taken off.

whole wheat The entire grain of wheat, which includes the outer layer (bran).

Equipment

non-stick baking sheet

cupcake liners

mixing bowl

grater

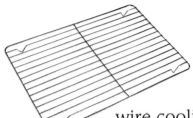
wire cooling rack

measuring cup

spatula

cutting board

mixing spoon

whisk

tablespoon

teaspoon

saucepan

colander

sharp knife

kitchen knife

frying pan

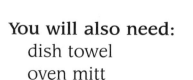
wooden spoons

You will also need:
dish towel
oven mitt

peeler

blender

food processor

Index

Activity Sheets

Request these free activity sheets at:
info@blackrabbitbooks.com

Pages 4–7 All about Lunch
Plan your lunches for the week ahead on this handy food chart. Fill in the shopping list so you know what you need to buy.

Pages 8–9 Sandwich Stacks
What sandwich fillings do your friends like best? Fill in this food survey to find out which are the most popular.

Page 31 Equipment
Download a colorful poster of all the equipment used in the *"Plan, Prepare, Cook"* books.